Jacky Newcomb is the UK's leading expert on the after-life, having dedicated her life to the subject. She is a *Sunday Times* bestselling author with numerous awards to her name, a regular columnist for *Take a Break*'s *Fate & Fortune* magazine, and a regular on ITV's *This Morning*. Jacky has also appeared on *Lorraine*, C5's *Live with Gabby* and *The Alan Titchmarsh Show*, among others.

Also by Jacky Newcomb:

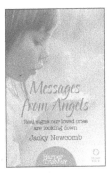

A Christmas
Angel

A Christmas Angel

True stories of gifts from angels at special times

Jacky Newcomb

Harper
True *Fate*

Some names have been changed
for privacy reasons

HarperTrueFate
An imprint of HarperCollins*Publishers*
1 London Bridge Street
London SE1 9GF

www.harpertrue.com
www.harpercollins.co.uk

First published by HarperTrueFate 2015

© Jacky Newcomb 2015

Jacky Newcomb asserts the moral right to
be identified as the author of this work

A catalogue record of this book is
available from the British Library

ISBN: 978-0-00-814443-2

Introduction

An angel is a common symbol at Christmas. I mean the gold and sparkly ones we use in decorations, of course! We place them on top of the Christmas tree; they decorate our Christmas cards and we light our candles in angel-themed holders. It was the Archangel Gabriel who told the young Mary that she was carrying a child. That child was the baby Jesus, and so Gabriel became known as the Christmas angel.

The angels were given the special task of watching over the small family on their journey to Bethlehem. One of them also told the shepherds that the Christ child had been born. Many witnessed the angels that day and readers of the Bible will recall that the poor shepherds were terrified at the sight. Much as I love angels, I'm sure I would have been just as frightened if several angels had suddenly appeared overhead while I walked with my sheep! Wonderful though their visit must have been, I'm sure the subtler visitations we experience today are much more comforting.

What is an angel or guardian angel? That question is on many people's lips. We have all seen angels represented in paintings, statues or figurines as winged beings or glowing figures, but is this who they really are?

Angels are said to be manifested by the divine being, the one true creator – or God, as we tend to call 'him'. It is said that God made the angels just before, or just after, he created humans (depending on which source you believe!). Some feel that God is an energy source (like a cloud of electricity), and all of his creations are like sub-clouds that separate from this heavenly being. Like drops of water in the ocean, we and the angels are not separate from each other or from God, but are all parts of the ocean, all parts of the energy cloud, all God. He/she is whole in all of us: in the souls on this side of life, in the souls on the heaven side of life, in the angels and in beings on other planets, too.

Many believe that angels watch over and guard us. But this is just one of the tasks they seem to take on. There are stories of their interactions with human lives that go back as far as you can imagine, before humans even began recording their history – whispered experiences passed down from one generation to the next.

While some don't believe they exist, these stories of angels interacting with human lives have been around for many thousands of years. If they are not real then why do people talk about meeting them, seeing them, hearing them or experiencing these beings of light? I am an 'experiencer'. I have been lucky enough to have a great deal of contact with God's angels. They have helped me and communicated with me many times. They reach out to us in their own way, and although contacting us through many different layers of consciousness can be a challenge, they still seem to manage it.

Some people believe that I personally hear and see angels all the time. This isn't true, sadly. I live a normal life; I'm a wife, mum and grandmother ('Nana Jacky!'), and on occasion I have had some unique, extraordinary experiences. Some might call them mind-blowing (I know I do). It seems to be no different for some of my readers. Some have more angelic contact than others, though there seems to be no specific reason why this might happen. Angels come when they want to and visit when we need them. Occasionally they appear when we ask them to, but sometimes they arrive unannounced. Always they are welcome. They seem to appear when we feel afraid or alone. We might not always see them (in fact, usually we don't), but if you are really lucky, you might sense them, hear them or pick up a little sign that they are there. Your angel is watching over you.

Can we really define an angel? Many have tried. They seem to be a type of spirit, but not like a human soul. They are beings of light but without solid bodies (or what we would call solid); they may not have a physical presence in our dimension, but they certainly have substance in their own realms. They exist, but on a different 'level' to the one where we humans live, and yet they seem to have the power to intervene in human lives. It's their divine and inspired role, their assigned task.

There are recorded stories of angels helping in war-torn areas, saving people from falling off cliffs and lifting cars in the air to a place of safety to avoid vehicle crashes. They've moved people away from out-of-control vehicles and urged them in another direction to keep them from getting hurt. They appear at the bedside of the sick and walk alongside those who are frightened or grieving. Some have felt them, some have smelt them, others have sensed their touch and many more have seen them.

Lots of people are happy to talk about their angel experiences. Many of their stories fill the pages of my books. Others are more reluctant. They feel their angel contact to have been nothing short of miraculous. They feel their experiences are to be whispered, treasured, as secret, private moments of pleasure and comfort, joy and peace. These people feel their encounters were meant just for them and them alone, and I respect that point of view ... But luckily for me, not everyone feels that way, and without these people there would be no books of angel experiences. I have always shared my own angel and afterlife visits with my readers. In fact, I feel I have been blessed with so many for that very reason: I was meant to share them. Telling the world about angel experiences, including my own, is my life's mission.

Your loving experiences come from all over the globe. There is no age barrier to having an encounter. Babies and the elderly see them equally. You may believe in angels or not – they still come to us in our time of need. Many start believing in angels only after they have had an encounter, which makes a lot of sense when these beings are so elusive in our day-to-day lives. It's truly a challenge to believe in something that you've had no contact with, or maybe no interest in, before. Some tell me that they want to believe in angels but aren't sure how they can make the leap between wanting to believe and believing. These books of angel experiences do help. It always amazes me that people who don't know each other, who have never met or spoken with each other, can have very similar experiences in their lives. They may come many years apart, and the individuals may have nothing in common at all, no shared interests, yet angels come to them in their hour of need. Their encounters may connect them at many different points.

I love to talk about my own angel visits … and there have been many. Angels often appear to me when I sleep. They also come to me when my body is relaxed in meditation. My mind works best when it's open to their contact, in an altered state of consciousness. This may also include the day-dreaming state we get into, when our minds are bored of what our hands are doing – they are fed up of making beds or washing up! People tell me they have extraordinary angel experiences while simply staring out of the window, wiping down a table or when their mind wanders during a boring speech. Your angel might reach out to you when you're waiting for your name to be called at the doctor's surgery or taking a bath or shower. They are waiting for us to idle our time away or mull something over. We create a little space in our waking consciousness for them to reach through and make their presence known. There is no perfect time, but lots of opportunity. Angels reach out to us in our time of need, when we are unsafe, sad or lonely. They are always here for us and inventive at finding out new ways to let us know.

Over the years I've recorded stories of angels helping humans in many ways. They love to help in times of danger but might also appear to simply hold your hand when you need a little reassurance. Your guardian angel (your personal guide and protector) will always be close by but will draw a little closer when you need support. Your angel is aware of the extremes of emotion we humans feel and will pick up on your energy when you are anxious, scared or unwell. During these occasions you are more likely to feel their presence. You may even hear them. Angel music (like a choir of harmonious voices) is an occasional gift from these loving beings. Angels use all of our human senses to make themselves known to us. Visually appearing to us (when we are awake) is the least likely way they will come to us (but surprisingly the way most people expect to encounter them, even though this would potentially be more frightening and less comforting!).

Our religious books show us that angels act as a contact between heaven and earth; they are a feature of many faiths. They reach up to God our creator to bring his messages down to earth to humankind – they are intermediaries and diplomats. There is even archaeological evidence for the existence of angels in earlier times. One appears in the form of a stele (a stone or wooden slab, carved and erected as a monument for commemorative purposes). This early carving commemorates King Ur-Nammu in Egypt (225BC) and in the image winged beings are shown flying over the king's head while he prays. Perhaps ancient people saw angels in their physical state just as it seems to show in the Bible. I guess we'll never know for sure.

Hopefully this latest collection of angelic experiences will open your mind a little more to the love that they bring us. Angels can draw close at any time, but these stories show how they visited during specific moments of importance. If you have had experiences like these, I'd love to hear from you. What do you think of these stories?

Chapter 1

Love and Valentines

Angels love to connect with us on special occasions in our lives. As humans we send out an energetic signature at these times that the other side picks up. Valentine's Day is no exception. Angels are part of much ancient religious symbolism. Even today, they appear in many forms for different occasions, like births, deaths (funerals) and, of course, Valentine's Day rituals. Cupid has become part of our culture, a traditional symbol that represents love. His image often appears on lovers' Valentine's cards alongside flowers and hearts.

I'm sure you are familiar with him – this cheeky little boy with wings is easily recognised with his bow and arrow: a baby angel! Lovers are often said to have been struck by Cupid's arrow. His image is now associated with love, passion, desire and attraction. Unsurprisingly, more than one online dating site uses the name Cupid. You can see why, can't you? Over the years, numerous people have written to tell me that they felt an angel, or a deceased loved one, help them find the love of their life.

I always felt I was struck by Cupid's arrow myself. This little cherub stabbed me with his arrow nearly 30 years ago. Sitting in a pub with my (then) boyfriend (let's call him 'M'), John (my now husband) walked in with a group of friends. They were having a lot of fun together, laughing and teasing each other. The group had been part of a local sports team and had just won a big game (I forget what they were playing, but it was probably hockey).

One of John's teammates picked me out and urged John to sit on my lap in the crowded bar; it was suggested as a type of bet and he duly did so. 1) My boyfriend 'M' was not amused. 2) Later I realised how out of character this act was for John. 3) I liked it! The strange thing was that as he sat on my lap (this almost-stranger whom I vaguely recognised from school), I heard a voice in my head say to me, 'This is the man you are going to marry!' No one could have been more surprised than me. Yet we didn't actually get together until a year later. We then dated for two years before we married; we chose the weekend closest to Valentine's Day (nowhere was available on the actual day – still, we tried!).

John and I have been married for over 30 years and I still tease him about that day. Even now he wonders how he had the nerve to do something so cheeky. Perhaps he, too, was encouraged in his behaviour by Cupid – our own loving angel! John has never been one for practical jokes; I always felt Cupid had hit us both with his arrow that day, although it seems that only I got the message from the angelic voice. Maybe only one of us needed to hear … I'm not complaining! Have you felt an angel, maybe Cupid himself, help connect you with your true love?

Karen had a very special 'someone' on the other side of life. Their relationship was difficult on the earth side of life because he was a public figure (and I'll still avoid using his name here out of respect for his memory). When he died, Karen and her love were able to be together … just in a different way. Over the years he acted as a guardian angel to her from the heaven side of life. As time went on she felt the connection grow between them. So strong was his spirit that she was able to ask for advice and 'hear' his answers. He would warn her when there was danger, comfort her when she felt sad and send her love when she needed it most. She called him her 'twin flame', her principal spirit guide.

There came a time when she was going through a failing marriage and facing uncertainty in the future. She feels that her twin flame, her loving spirit friend, supported her during this difficult time. One day – she remembers the date clearly: 13 February 2007 – she went to bed as usual, but this was going to be no ordinary night. Something happened that would change her life forever.

Karen was not looking forward to the next day when all of her friends and family would be celebrating St Valentine's Day. It took her a long time to settle, and just as she was starting to relax, she felt her spirit-self drifting off out of her body. This phenomenon is not common, but some people experience the separation of the spirit and body during meditation or when the body is deeply relaxed (or sometimes when the body is in trauma). Occasionally it can happen when the body is asleep. It's happened to me on numerous occasions. Different to a dream, you can remain totally aware as you go on to have a spiritual (or mystical) experience. And unlike a dream, you remember it fully when you wake.

Now 'out of body', Karen looked down from where her spirit-self had drifted, which appeared to be up on the ceiling. Her physical body was just lying there in the bed below; after some moments she felt herself floating up even higher and then away from her bedroom completely. Almost immediately she was looking down at her favourite reservoir close to her home in South Wales; it's so beautiful, she explained to me, that it's more like a scenic lake than a reservoir. It was like the most powerful dream, yet so real. She was totally aware during the whole thing ... lucid, and thinking normally. Only the experience was extraordinary.

A Christmas Angel

One minute Karen was in bed, and the next she was looking down on this watery scene!

Karen felt herself swooping downwards and landing on the shore below her. She remembers that she was wearing a beautiful flowing white gown, which had several layers and tiers of fabric, and she says she felt fabulous! In front of her were two groups of people waiting at the reservoir edge, but she couldn't make out who they were. Then she found herself walking over towards them, and as she got close she realised that one group was her dad and other family members who had died, and the other group was her 'twin flame's' dad and his family (the family of her lost love on the other side of life). They were all smiling at her as if they had been waiting to welcome her for this visit. She recalls that it was a beautiful, peaceful atmosphere. There was a bright light a little way across the shore where she could see two silhouettes, but again she couldn't make out who they were. Karen's dad took her by the arm and led her towards the light – and it was then that she realised that one of the silhouettes was her beloved, and the other was her guardian angel.

Karen was delighted as her special love took her hand. He looked so happy that it brought her to tears. The experience was so vivid that Karen immediately asked if she was dead, but her angel told her, 'Absolutely not!' The next thing she remembers is being told that she and her man were to have a blessing ceremony. The angel explained that it was like a spiritual wedding between twin flames for when one is in spirit (heaven) and the other is in the physical realm (earth).

This extraordinary experience was now happening on Valentine's Day and the significance of it wasn't lost on Karen. They – the angels – explained that the ritual was to prevent anything or anyone ever coming between them, and that they'd never lose each other again. The death of one partner didn't sever the spirit connection between them. Once the ceremony had been performed they'd be 'married' for all eternity, and when it was eventually Karen's 'time' (to cross over to the other side for good), they would be reunited and never parted again. The whole thing seemed like a fairy tale, but it was real.

Karen was asked if she wanted to proceed, and she remembers being so excited and wanting it to go ahead immediately. Her guardian angel proceeded to talk to them both and read some words from a white book; all the while Karen and her loved one were holding hands and looking into each other's eyes. A golden cord was placed over their hands to connect them forever, and she recalls at this point that the angel closed his eyes as if he were praying. The ceremony seemed surreal yet perfect. It was more powerful than any dream, more real than even a waking experience, and she knew something amazing had happened between them. When she awoke the next morning, on Valentine's Day, she was finally content. She had a connection with her loved one like none of her friends – the angels had seen to that. In so many ways, Valentine's Day is now more important to Karen than to anyone she knows. This special date marks the anniversary of her spiritual wedding!

Not long after this episode, Karen and her children finally moved out of the family home into rented accommodation. The long-awaited divorce from her earthly husband followed and life settled down again. Her heavenly twin flame/spiritual husband has been there to support her the whole time. Karen took her commitment one step further. One night soon afterwards he appeared to her in a dream, asking her to change her surname to his, 'now that they were married', and to wear a 'commitment' ring for him in place of her old earthly wedding ring, which she'd recently removed. She was only too happy to do so and went straight to town and ordered one in her size, and when she returned she applied online to change her surname legally.

Karen explained that the process took several days, because things had to be signed and witnessed, but the very day her name-change certificate arrived and she was officially and legally able to use her new surname, she got a text to say that her ring was ready.

Divine timing! Karen has worn the ring ever since. Her spirit husband says they will still have a 'proper' wedding when they are reunited in heaven, and he's promised he will replace the commitment ring with a wedding ring and an eternity ring – although Karen says that as far as they are concerned they are already married, and she couldn't be happier under the circumstances.

Her story is pretty extraordinary, and it's rare for someone to have such a close connection to the heaven side of life that it almost feels as if the loved one is still here. Their time on earth has been far too short – in this lifetime. But like many these days, Karen understands that this is one of many lives we live. We are born, we live, we die and we return to the heavenly side of life. More and more people tell me about visits (spirit visitations) they've had from the afterlife. My family and I have had (and still have) so much contact from my late father that we wrote a book about it. The angels are there to help create the connection, often ushering spirits forward, providing energy to make the connection. It sounds surreal ... but it's real. They bring us information about what the future holds (when they are permitted), but they also show us they are around when we are going through difficult times in our lives. I wonder if many of us have soul connections with husbands and wives on the other side of life. Having the psychic ability to connect in this way would comfort so many.

A Christmas Angel

Our deceased loved ones can often appear during special loving events. Wedding anniversaries, for example. Els's grandparents have both passed away. She says that in each case she knew about it deep inside before being told by anyone; it was as if their souls somehow brought the news to her. The day her granddad died, she told me that her watch stopped at the exact time of his passing. But when her grandmother died, as well as the usual sadness she had the most extraordinary experience. She told me, 'I felt a very strong, tender warmth in my body.' Els's grandmother had managed to make contact right after her soul left her physical body, and amazingly Els says she can still feel her grandparents from time to time.

Then recently she was attending her uncle and aunt's 40th wedding anniversary party. Els was looking at some photographs and took the opportunity to ask about the family who had already passed over. She told me that when she asked her cousins to share some memories about their grandparents (both deceased at the time of the party), she felt the presence of their spirit behind her. Els's grandparents may well have already drawn close for the party. I believe our loved ones on the other side of life continue to attend special family events when they can (weddings, christenings and all manner of family get-togethers).

If you take a photograph at your yearly barbecue, don't be surprised if you notice an orb-like light appearing in shot. It could well be the spirit of a loving relative who just wants to join in the fun … especially if they were always the life and soul of any event when on the earth side of life. I know that if I was on the heaven side of life, I'd take the opportunity of visiting loved ones on occasions when several family and friends were gathered together, especially if this was something you'd done in life. Next time you have a gathering of loved ones, don't forget to invite 'absent friends'! If you're feeling brave, ask them to let you have a sign of their presence, too. It might seem scary, but actually it shouldn't be. That loving energy they brought you in life is still the same after the passing of the physical body. The love never changes and the energy vibration of that love 'feels' exactly the same. It's the idea of the contact that brings fear; the actual contact is amazing!

Christine wrote to tell me about a 1940s revival weekend that she attended with her son and family. The event brought back memories of her late mother, because of course it was an era that she was a part of for real. She would have been 20 years old at the time.

Christine explained that her mum had passed on over 10 years ago and she was thinking of her the whole time she was at the event. She says that as she stood eating and looking around she felt a connection with how her mum must have felt at the time … while the war was going on around her. The sounds, the smells, the dress; it aligned their energies from heaven and earth for a brief moment. It was at that time, that exact time, that she made a connection with her mum. It happened suddenly, and she felt her mum's presence surround her with so much love and hug her. Her mum's spirit had felt the call from earth and was now standing with Christine in that very room. Christine was so overcome with emotion that she burst into tears of happiness. It felt like a big weight had been lifted from her shoulders. Her mum was okay and she was right there with her.

Christine was aware that others might see her mum's spirit, and her son could certainly see that something strange was going on! When he asked her why she was crying she explained that it was because she felt that his nana was with them and she was so glad to have stepped into the deceased woman's memories. Right away her tears stopped and she was no longer upset. Christine was left with wonderful memories and a truly beautiful and loving experience from her late mother. I'm sure the connection left them both feeling deeply at peace.

I love this. I think Christine's mum chose the perfect occasion to reach out from heaven. Love crosses all boundaries, and that 'day dreaming' state of mind provides the perfect opportunity for our loved ones to reach us. I once had a similar experience, which you may have read about in an earlier book. I remember being at a venue when the Battle of Britain planes flew overhead. The trio of planes, the same famous fighter aircraft used in the Second World War air campaign of 1940, included the British Hawker Hurricane, Lancaster and Spitfire; they were special in the hearts of many who took part in the war. I was musing over how much my late father and his brother would have loved to witness the event and how proud they would have felt seeing the planes in the sky still, after all these years.

It was at that moment I made a similar connection to Christine and felt surrounded by the most over-powering sense of love. It was so strong that I, too, burst into tears. At once I felt my father, uncle and father-in-law surround me – one at each side and one behind me. I was unable to do anything but cry for several minutes, at one point trying to hide in a corner from the people walking by. I felt embar-rassed but was unable to stop the flow of tears. My poor husband found me and was thoroughly concerned when he saw me; I was unable to explain and he quickly ushered me into the car.

Then the feeling lifted and the tears disappeared. I felt that my loved ones had pulled their energy back, and with that the overpowering feeling of love now became a gentle, warm vibration. When we looked at our morning, everything became clear. John and I had planned to visit this location fairly early in the day, but our plans had been thwarted by numerous silly things that kept causing delays to our trip. It took longer and longer for us to leave the house, to the point where we almost decided not to go at all. Of course, in the end, we realised the whole thing was perfectly timed – you could say it was divine timing. If we hadn't arrived when we did, it's unlikely we would still have been at the venue at the time when the planes passed over. I guess our loved ones had it all worked out in advance.

Isn't it strange how our heavenly beings (both angels and deceased loved ones) seem able to arrange these magical events? They can come to us in dream visitations or just bring a loving hug or touch. It's possible to feel that touch physically (a hand upon a shoulder, for example, or their hand holding yours). You might feel a celestial hug or an overpowering sense of love from heaven, as both Christine and I were lucky enough to receive.

I must warn you, though: the loving feeling is all-encompassing. It can be overwhelming and, as I said above, both embarrassing and wonderful at the same time! Maybe you'll make that connection with an angel or a deceased loved one and experience something similar. It's a memory that I shall treasure forever. If you'd like contact like this, I would suggest you talk about loving experiences you have shared while sitting at home with other family members. It's certainly less embarrassing than crying in public! But perhaps that doesn't matter at all.

Chapter 2

Angels and Christmas

At such a special time of year, when angels are visible all around us – looking down from the top of the Christmas tree, appearing as a message of hope and love on Christmas cards from loved ones and in the Christmas carols we sing – it's unsurprising that we feel they are even closer than at other times of the year. Christmas is a period when emotions are heightened and the loss of those we love can be more difficult to cope with.

One Christmas, Joyce and her husband were talking about her husband's late sister, Joyce's sister-in-law. She explained to me how their Christmas tree used to shake whenever they spoke about their relative, almost as if the very fact of talking about the deceased woman drew her spirit close. On the anniversary of her passing, in the early hours of the morning, a box fell off the top of the cupboard and made everyone jump. But that wasn't the end of the story ... Inside the box was a china angel. It certainly sounds as if this lovely lady wanted to be noticed.

A Christmas Angel

What a clever symbol! Spirits love to let us know that they are still around and that they are our 'angels' in heaven now, keeping a close check on our lives on earth. I always welcome visits from my own family of angels on the other side of life, particularly at this special time of year. So many of us connect with our relations at this time, making us also more aware of the gap in our lives left by the passing of loved ones in previous years.

Vicky's story is especially poignant. I first met Vicky at a mind, body and spirit show back in 2011. Vicky had given birth to her little girl Ellie the year before, but tragically, due to complications, the little one passed away at birth. The whole family was devastated, as you can imagine.

Angels were keen to reassure Vicky that her little girl was safely with them, and the day before the funeral she felt that the Archangel Gabriel was with her. The Christmas angel was the perfect visitor for the grieving mother – a gentle energy connecting with her in a loving way. Although we can't always explain why or how, you always know when an angel is nearby. You just pick up on their presence. Their connection is without words; they and we just don't need them at this time. Their energy is clear, pure and full of joy and comfort. Your body recognises the signature they bring.

Then, on Christmas Day, later in the same year we'd met, Vicky was standing at the foot of her little girl's grave, feeling the full force of her grief. It was a very bad day indeed. Vicky says she was sobbing her heart out when she decided to walk to the top of her little princess's grave and light a tea light in the lantern she had placed there. Then, as she went back to the foot of the grave, right in front of her eyes a lovely white feather appeared. Immediately she was surrounded by a feeling of great calmness and her tears stopped. She told me, 'I felt like I was embraced and held in the arms of such calmness and tranquillity, to the point where I actually began to smile, knowing I'd received a blessing.' I recognised this experience at once – one that brings a different type of tears, followed my smiles.

Nothing can take away the pain of losing a child, but an angel sign can bring a little comfort. Vicky felt she'd received a sign that day. The feeling she experienced reminds me of the loving hugs I wrote about earlier. The awe-inspiring emotion seems to come from both our passed-over relatives and the angels – probably at the same time. They also possess a sort of healing energy that seems to sweep over us, helping to mend a broken heart. Anyone privileged enough to have felt this will certainly know what I mean.

Alison shared a warning experience she had with her own angel. She explained that she was out shopping for Christmas cards four years ago and was searching for a special card for her mum. Suddenly she heard a voice in her right ear say, 'She won't be here at Xmas.' At the time she thought it strange and couldn't shake off what she'd heard. Tragically, just one week later her mum had a stroke, and a week and a half after that she sadly passed away.

Sad though this experience was, Alison tells me that, had it not been for that loving warning message in her ear, she feels sure she would have had trouble coping. At the funeral, both her husband and brother broke down in tears, but Alison felt she had to hold it together for them, and her earlier contact brought her ease. Alison is so grateful for her angelic voice and says that overall she feels the experience made her a much stronger person. She thanks the wonderful angels for their good work and the help that they impart to everyone, and welcomes the angels into her heart.

On Christmas Day 2009, Michelle's granddad was taken into hospital. For months he'd been suffering with cancer and the disease was spreading through his body. Sadly, just two weeks later he passed away. The family scattered his ashes near a holiday park not far from Poole in Dorset.

Then a year later the family went back to the area, to honour his memory. Michelle took two white roses with her to place on a commemorative bench; it was an area her granddad had loved and he used to take vacations in the family caravan there. Then she explained what happened next: 'We were all sitting

Jacky Newcomb

on and standing around the bench near the sea, and out of nowhere a beautiful robin came and sat right next to my uncle. It stayed with us for ages.' The bird seemed special, and extra brave. Its presence seemed to touch the family and they agreed they all felt great comfort at the gift, feeling that the robin was a sign that 'Grampy' was with them and watching over them still.

I love Michelle's experience. Birds are common signs of spirit visits (along with butterflies, dragonflies and occasionally moths) and seem to appear as messengers when a family are in mourning. Robins in particular are a regular sight, and depending on what part of the world you live in, hummingbirds are another special treat. I live at the seaside and the seagulls here are usually just annoying, but one reader told me recently of an experience she'd had where a seagull appeared on numerous occasions that were linked to spirit contact. Have you ever received a bird sign from the afterlife? I've asked that blue tits (a common species in my area of the world) knock on my window to show me that heaven and the afterlife is real. I've never been disappointed!

When a loved one dies on Christmas Day itself the loss seems even more tragic. But in so many ways it is a day of love and family. Michael wrote to tell me about his father, who passed away on Christmas Day 1998. After he died, Michael's mum, sister and brother all claimed to have seen Dad in visitation dreams; his spirit came to visit them while they slept. This kind of spirit visit is quite common – the soul finds it easier to see us when our bodies are asleep, and we are more able to accept the encounters. The dreams are vivid and we are lucid, and when we awake the memory stays fresh in our minds – very different from a dream.

Michael was sad because he hadn't had a visit. He suggests it might be because of the challenges he was experiencing in his life at the time of his dad's passing. Several years later he says his life came together more and he was in a better place. It was at this time that his dad appeared in a special dream type of visit. Michael wrote: 'Dad showed me that, now he was in heaven, he was aware of what I had done in my life, and I could sense his disappointment.' Michael took the opportunity to apologise to his father ... and also wondered how his dad was able to speak to him now he was dead! His dad smiled and said he'd been given permission to help 'fix' things for him.

After the visitation experience, Michael says his life really started to change for the better. He is now in a new relationship, with two wonderful stepchildren; he says he loves that the children view him as 'Dad', not a stepdad. Maybe this is what his dad meant by fixing things ... Life still has its ups and downs, but Michael feels that maybe he doesn't have to feel guilty about his past any more. He has been forgiven.

Of course, we all make mistakes, but correcting them is the best way forward. An apology goes a long way to solving the issue, and I know I sleep better at night knowing I have done my best for the people I have wronged. Even if the person you hurt is on the other side, it's never too late. I often hear stories of spirits coming back from heaven to apologise, or of us apologising to them and then receiving a visit to let us know they have got the message. It's rather wonderful, isn't it?

Lynn explained how her husband Garry had passed away from lung and bone cancer back in December 2009. It was close to Christmas and he was only 53 years old. Lynn was devastated and felt very alone. Then a few days after he died she was lying in bed when she heard her late husband call her name. It was definitely his voice and it rang out loud and clear. I don't know if anyone else has had this experience, but there is no mistaking a spirit voice. Several times I've been woken up myself by the voice of a passed-over loved one calling my name, and on at least one occasion I was wide awake when it happened. From everything the spirits have told me, it takes some serious effort to create the phenomenon, so the voice was a very loving sign.

Another time soon after, Lynn was asleep on the living-room sofa when she was woken by the unmistakable sound of bells; they jingled and shook in the room. Lynn wasn't frightened by the experience and just drifted back off to sleep. The bells had been hanging on the Christmas tree in the room, but when she woke up that morning they were on the floor. Lynn swears she hadn't heard them drop to the floor ... and yet the floor is laminated, a hard surface. You'd think they would make a very loud noise indeed.

Then a few weeks later she was again woken up from her sleep. Just above her eyeline the air in the room was filled with patterns of red and white stripes. The patterns seemed to stick around for about a minute or so before disappearing. Garry was buried in his favourite football shirt: a Stoke City shirt, and the red and white stripes feature in the team logo. It was a unique and clever sign from heaven. Lynn knows the experience was real and says she got straight out of bed afterwards.

I am delighted to tell you that Lynn has recently remarried. Her new partner's wife passed away just three weeks after her own husband. One day the woman came to her in a real dream visit or spirit visitation. She just wanted to let Lynn know that she thought she was okay. It seems that Lynn had been 'checked out' by the spirit from the other side of life, and thankfully the spirit woman approved of her old husband's new wife!

Jen sent me a delightful experience, which I'd love to share with you here. She explained that she'd just finished reading my book, *An Angel Held My*

Hand. She read it with an open mind, not really having thought about the existence of angels in much depth before. She'd believed in spirits for a while and thought that we possibly all have a guardian angel, but had never considered what else that might mean.

Reading my book got her thinking, but still she wasn't totally convinced. Jen explained that she'd had 'unexplained' things happen to her in the past and wanted to share this with us. The most memorable, she recalls, was when she was lying in bed one night. Suddenly she could 'see' her nan, although she says she can't fully explain what it was like. She was there, right in front of her, but not in a physical sense. She asked, 'Nan? What are you doing here?' and sat up, thinking she would be gone, but for a few more moments she stayed with Jen until she vanished as quickly as she'd arrived. Jen didn't think too much about it, other than the fact that it was a weird experience. The next morning Jen's mum phoned her to say that her nan had passed away; it was only a few days before her 90th birthday. She was never close to her nan and had no idea why she chose to visit her that night, but it was something she feels privileged to have experienced.

Loved ones can pop over to say goodbye in their spirit form. Some of my older books contain stories of children whose grandparents say goodbye just before they leave the earth plane. It's not only children who do this, but they do seem more open to the phenomenon. If you consider the 'special occasions' theme of this book as a whole, I guess there is nothing more important than the day we transition from one form of existence to another: our 'birth' (or perhaps rebirth) into a heavenly form once more. Sometimes the loved one appears alone (as happened in Jen's case) but usually there is another figure in the vision, either that of an angel or a being who appears as an assistant (carrying suitcases for the long journey ahead, for example) or just in a supporting role, as a spiritual guide. The other being appears to be helping to 'hold the energy' needed to make the goodbye visit possible. I love these stories.

When her dad passed away in 2009 Jen was distraught and missed him so much. Just before Christmas, 10 months after he'd died, Jen and her husband were at a garden centre. 'I wanted something to put on Dad's grave but just could not decide what to get. I didn't want a wreath but didn't know what I did want. Eventually we settled on a little fir tree in a green bucket.' The bucket was traction-engine green, and her dad loved traction engines. The couple paid for the tree and went back to the car, but as it was just before Christmas the car park was packed. Her husband complained that it would take ages to get out, so Jen told him to drive to the end of the section they were in, as she was sure someone would let them out into the queue. Sure enough, they did. As the couple looked at the car in front they immediately noticed the number plate – DAD! Maybe her dad was saying he approved of the little fir tree.

After that Jen kept seeing car number plates with DAD on them. Having established 'their sign', her dad repeated the experience as often as he could. It always seemed to happen when Jen particularly missed him, like his birthday or Father's Day or any time she thought of him.

One day, after seeing their special sign, Jen said, 'Dad, if this is you sending me these number plates, send me another one.' Sure enough, on her return journey she spotted another one. Dad was a motor mechanic so cars were his life, and Jen has Asperger's syndrome so she tells me that number patterns (in particular, number plates) are something of particular interest to her. She's always trying to make words from them, so it's fitting that her dad let her know he was still around in that way.

I love number-plate signs and often see them. Sometimes I sense my father-in-law around and then immediately afterwards notice his initials in a number plate. Occasionally I spot Dad, too, and it's always when I feel him around us. On the day we moved into one of our old houses I found a white feather on the doormat, and on our first trip out I spotted a van with the word DAD on the side. I knew he had helped us to find the house, and we were very happy there.

Why don't you watch out for number-plate signs, too? You might also spot a poster with an important message or read a passage in a book or magazine that feels especially significant to you. Words in print are just one of many ways in which loved ones reach out to us.

Natalia is from Poland, and she immediately apologised for her English (I don't speak other languages myself, apart from a little I learned at school). But language ability never stops a good angel story (I often use an internet translation program to read stories in foreign tongues). Natalia contacted me after reading one of my books, when she recalled an encounter of her own.

After her mum died (at the very young age of 25) when Natalia was just six years old, Natalia used to communicate with her mum in her mind. When she was 18 years old she'd reach out to her mum with her thoughts and say to her, 'When you're here, please touch my hand.' Natalia was amazed when she always felt the sensation of a responding touch on her hand!

She recalls a lot of activity immediately after the funeral in particular. She explained how 'strange things' would happen at home. Once, at night, she picked up the very strong scent of her mother's favourite perfume. Natalia is now 21 years old and the visits have slowed right down. She misses her mum being around in the way that she once was. Some time ago she miscarried a baby and longed for her mother to take care of her child. After this tragedy, her mum appeared in a dream visit to Natalia's husband. She told him that another child was on its way and that this time all would be well. Natalia's husband had never met her mother, so it seemed unusual that she chose to visit in this way. Then a month later the pair discovered that Natalia was pregnant again. They now have a healthy daughter – she was born on Christmas Eve. A wonderful gift. She finished by saying that my book had changed her life, and I was so glad it had helped to bring her comfort. Congratulations to them both.

I was sad to hear that Janeine's mother had passed away just a week before she wrote to me. Since then the family had experienced several signs from the mother's spirit. One was that her dad's Rolex watch had stopped working unexpectedly. Then her son-in-law's doorbell rang one day, and no one was there. I love spiritual doorbell-ringers and have many doorbells ring (with no one there) at my own home. Janeine was upstairs at home reading a prayer the vicar had dropped round. For no particular reason, the lights blew in the room with a bang and a flash. When I read this I recalled having a similar experience with my own family. Following requests for contact from my late uncle, the light began flickering in my sister's kitchen where we were all gathered at the time. Then the bulb literally exploded out of the socket, plunging the room into darkness. Luckily we all burst out laughing. No one was frightened and we all considered it a great joke. I'm sure our uncle was just trying to signal with the light, not blow it. Later on he got really good at just flickering, so we never had another breakage after this.

When Janeine went downstairs later she reached over to turn on the Christmas tree lights. This time all the house lights went out. Janeine reasoned that her mum had loved Christmas and was convinced that she was letting her know she was okay. It's a fun story. Would you feel comfortable with flickering lights as a sign from your own loved ones?

Like Michael, Julie's family also suffered a tragedy on Christmas Day when her own father passed away. Her very sad story also has a shining message or two. Julie tells me she has always been a massive believer in the afterlife and angels. Her dad, on the other hand, was very sceptical and often used to joke about it. On Christmas Eve 2011, the family were all gathered at her parents' home when her dad suddenly became very poorly and the family had to call an ambulance. It looked like he was having a heart attack. The paramedics were marvellous and although nothing showed up on the heart monitor he was admitted to hospital just to be on the safe side. After lots of tests it was decided to keep him in overnight as a precaution; a blood test 12 hours later would determine if he actually had suffered a heart attack. Julie's mum gave him a packet of tissues, and he noticed the white feather printed on the packet and pointed it out. He took it seriously when Julie explained that feathers were an angelic calling card and it meant the angels were going to look after him. The family couldn't have imagined they were taking care of him the way they did, though …

They planned to pick him up early on Christmas morning so he could supervise the cooking of the dinner (he was always the chef!). Unfortunately their world was shattered when a phone call at 6:30 a.m. told them to hurry to the hospital, as he had taken a turn for the worse. Julie's dad had already passed away when they got there. To say they were shattered was an understatement; they were absolutely devastated.

Christmas Day went in a blur of sadness and tears. Even now Julie still can't believe it happened the way it did. Her daughter Zoe fell asleep on the settee for a few hours that day, and when she woke up, underneath her was a pure white feather. Julie's mum made her open a special present that her dad had chosen for her – unbelievably it was a silver necklace with angel wings! Julie and her daughter decided to stay at her mum's that night and then early the following morning they popped home for a change of clothes. Even before she unlocked her front door, she says she spotted a beautiful red admiral butterfly right there on the windowsill and felt immediately that it was a sign from her dad. He was a gardener and used to talk about a robin that would often sit on his spade at his allotment. From 27 December, Julie saw robins all the time, and to this day one regularly appears in their garden.

Birds and butterflies are wonderful signs that spirits are around us, and Julie says that from then on she saw them everywhere. Everything from sympathy cards to gifts from friends had either butterflies, robins or white feathers on them. She ordered a couple of my books, she told me, and couldn't believe some of the coincidences she was experiencing and then reading about. On the day the books arrived she was listening to the *City of Angels* movie soundtrack. She particularly recalls her dad's birthday. She and her mum went to the crematorium for the first time since he had passed. They have CCTV on their driveway, which her partner checks now and again. He noticed what could only be described as a fairy, and it flew right across the screen. She believes it was a definite sign from her dad, letting them know he was still around. Julie's mum has apparently had a couple of signs herself. She regularly picks up the scent of his deodorant, and she even saw him briefly once! Just recently, she was 100 per cent certain that he kissed her when she lay in bed. Isn't that wonderful?

I am always overwhelmed at spirit contact; it seems both imaginative and spectacular. I often felt Dad's hands in mine both when he was ill (when he was in a coma) and after he passed. Dad had big, strong, healing hands (I included a photograph of his hand on one of my afterlife cards: 'Messages from Heaven'). His hands were very distinctive and since he has passed I sometimes see and feel his hands holding mine before I'm aware of anything else. That spirit touch, which feels so physical and human, is amazing. How do they do that?

Melanie would often see what she describes as 'flashes' of her nan when she was least expecting it. She would appear at the bottom of the stairs, watching her, or in front of her when she was working on a project. She could feel her presence very strongly at unexpected times. The loveliest experience she ever had was when she was lying in bed one Saturday morning. She'd been awake for ages, reading and thinking about her. She was mulling over how much she loved and missed her when suddenly the room filled with a strange feeling of what she described as pure love and forgiveness. Melanie felt she was enveloped in it for several minutes before it went away, and then sensed the atmosphere change again. A part of her was very sad when she lost that feeling. It made her want to cry, but with tears of both sadness and happiness. That 'feeling' sounds familiar by now, doesn't it? It keeps appearing in stories over and over again.

Melanie recalls one occasion when she was very upset and says that she sent out a prayer for her nan's help. Thirty seconds later the telephone rang – her boyfriend wanted to know if she was okay, because he had a strange feeling that she needed him! Isn't that clever? Melanie's nan managed to encourage her boyfriend to ring and check up on her.

Last Christmas Eve Melanie went to her nan's grave and as she stood there she cried heavily. Like most of us, Melanie misses her loved one so much, even to this day (she died 29 years ago!). But as she stood there, for no clear reason she was suddenly filled with absolute calm and realised that her nan was standing right there next to her. She felt a gentle pressure surrounding her, as though her nan were giving her a hug. She asked outright if it was really her. Then just as suddenly she was flooded with memories of events they had shared that Melanie hadn't thought of in years. She recalled one day when they had stopped for a cheese and onion pie, and the pie had no filling! She remembered her nan giving her stamp collection to her granddaughter, and one of the few times she was ever really naughty. Then there was the memory of when a sheep ate her sandwich! The memories rolled over Melanie, one at a time. They were just random things, normal every-day things … things that connected her to her nan.

Eventually she felt she had to move on, but beforehand she had another job to do. Melanie asked her nan to guide her to her uncle's grave – a spot where she'd never been before. To her surprise she found it straight away (which had also happened the first time she went to her nan's grave, 15 years after she'd died!). She told both her nan and her uncle that the best sign she could have – to let her know that she wasn't imagining their presence – would be snow on Christmas Day, which so rarely happens. Now, Melanie says she knows spirits are not responsible for the weather, but at eight o'clock on Christmas Day evening the family were outside playing in a thick blanket of snow! Wonderful!

Here is another Christmas-related experience. Tracy told me that her dad felt a spirit brush past him in their house one year, but that wasn't the only trick the spirit had up its sleeve. A few Christmases ago, her mum was putting up the decorations, and this included two battery-operated candles. She stood them by the fire but didn't have any of the correct-sized batteries to put in them, so she just displayed them without. Then later that evening Tracy explained that the candles lit up by themselves – without batteries! I wonder if the spirit visitor was a loved one or just an angel popping by to check that everything was okay. It's a little spooky – but in a good way.

Danielle told me how she saw her grandfather arrive as a mist after he passed away (I wrote up her story for a magazine article many years ago). She explained that her granddad had had a heart attack but seemed to have made a good recovery. The day before he died Danielle felt an urgent need to go and visit him. Her grandma was out shopping when she arrived but her granddad received her with open arms and they talked for over an hour. When she left they hugged and kissed. It almost seemed like she was saying a final goodbye at the time, and then she realised the importance of this opportunity afterwards.

When Danielle awoke the next morning she was in a very cheerful mood. Something attracted her attention and she looked up at the ceiling. It was then that she saw a slight hazy mist above her head. Later that day she received the dreadful call to tell her that her granddad had died. Naturally she was devastated. He'd looked so well and it really caught her by surprise. Looking back, she realised why she'd seen the mist. Her granddad had wanted to let his granddaughter know that he was okay, even though he had left his physical body. But this wasn't the end of the story ...

Christmas was fast approaching and a month later, on Christmas Eve, the young woman drove to her local supermarket to buy some last-minute Christmas presents. She was really excited about the things she'd bought and actually began opening the packages and wrapping the presents in the car.

Danielle confessed, 'I know it was wrong of me but when I had finished, I threw the bag outside, underneath my car, so no one would see!'

She had other plans and rushed off to meet friends, but when she went to hand over her credit card to pay for her lunch she realised that her card was missing. She was frantic, but the first thing she thought was: would Granddad be able to help? It was worth asking. It was then that she had a sort of feeling, a type of vision. She saw the image of her credit card in the carrier bag and admits, 'I guess it was my own fault!' Danielle rushed back to the car park, all the while thinking how she would have to cancel her credit card and how inconvenient that would be at Christmas. But lo and behold, as she drove into the car park, the exact same driving space was there waiting for her. A carrier bag was blowing up against the kerb, and inside was the missing bank card!

Danielle's friends kept saying, 'How lucky is that?' But she knew differently. Luck had had nothing to do with it. Her granddad was watching over things from the other side and had helped her out after she'd requested he do so. Her granddad may have left his physical body, but he hadn't gone far away after all.

I wonder if, because we open our hearts at Christmas and are more spiritually aware and uplifted, it can make us more psychic at this time.

A Christmas Angel

Although this isn't an angel story, I thought I would still include it here as it did make me laugh. Mary told me: 'At Christmas a few years ago I was eating my meal with the family, and I saw the TV presenter and decorating expert Laurence Llewelyn-Bowen clearly in my dinner plate. Everyone laughed at me.' Later that day the family were watching presenter Noel Edmonds doing a review on his television show when, out of the blue, Laurence Llewelyn-Bowen appeared out of a washing machine (which was the way Noel's guests came on)! Noel was astonished and asked him what he was doing there, and Laurence explained that he'd happened to be in the studio and decided to say hello. Mary was stunned at how she had seen such a similar vision earlier in the day – the white roundness of the plate seemed so similar to the circle of the washing-machine door on the television programme.

Our minds work in such mysterious ways. Has your mind ever picked up psychic senses or spirit contact when you were relaxed and having fun? Most of my psychic experiences like this are just as random.

Chapter 3

Births, Birthdays and Deaths

Katie was feeling really low on her birthday one year. She found herself single after being in a turbulent relationship, but says her heart felt as though it had been smashed into a million pieces. Although Katie's family and friends had bought her lovely gifts and were doing everything they could to lift her spirits, she still felt deeply unhappy inside.

Silently, she decided to ask the angels to give her a clear sign that they were still with her, although she worried she'd get no sign at all. But as the distressed woman stepped outside on that beautifully sunny and dry day, she looked up into the sky to see the most miraculous sight: above the house was one little white fluffy cloud. And in the middle was a rainbow!

Katie says that rainbows have always been one of her favourite things, and the sight of it was like a sprinkling of angel dust over her day. She knew then that she would never be alone. 'My angels would always be with me, loving me unconditionally. It's something I've never forgotten ...' she confides.

I love rainbows, and they are often seen by people asking for a sign. I recall the morning of Dad's funeral. It had been sunny first thing in the morning, but just as we left the house it began to rain. It was that very fine kind of rain, but it didn't last very long. In fact, it lasted just long enough for the family to drive round to Mum and Dad's house where a big rainbow sat, right over the top of the house! Have you ever seen a rainbow after asking for an angel sign? They are always so magical and uplifting, aren't they?

Claire feels a regular presence watching over her while she sleeps. She sometimes wakes in the night and senses their calm presence. Although this has happened a few times, she says the most memorable occasion was a few weeks before she discovered she was pregnant with her first child. That night she woke to see colours hovering over her; they vanished when she sat up.

Claire explained: 'Having my son changed my life for the better, as I suffer from Crohn's disease and was really struggling with my health at that time.' She feels the encounter was a sign to say that things would get better, and they did.

Her experience happened at a time when she was feeling very alone and down. The illness seemed to cut her off from the rest of the world. She lost her confidence and didn't go out much, but following her experience she felt encouraged to find out more about angels. They gave Claire strength and courage, and she feels they brought her son as a gift. 'The angels gave me hope and love and my son. They saved my life and I am thankful every day.' Having a baby meant that Claire was almost forced into going out and being sociable again. A baby has many needs, so the mother has the perfect reason to leave the house, and random strangers love to peer into a pushchair and admire the baby. Good luck to them both.

My dad passed over many years ago, but since he died he has come back as a spirit to communicate with numerous members of my family and even old friends of his. His communication has never ceased, but it does go quiet from time to time. He will sometimes leave signs to show that he has visited; I remember one occasion when the family was gathered together and talking about Dad when an old favourite song of his suddenly played in the restaurant where we were eating. All of the songs played up till then had been current ones, so this song, by The Carpenters – a Seventies group – seemed out of place. But any song by The Carpenters was never going to be out of favour with Dad.

Most regularly, though, Dad appears in dreams, in what I call spirit visitations. Sometimes we might be having an ordinary dream, but this moves to one side to be replaced by Dad walking in through a door and just chatting with us about the family. He makes it clear that he is watching over us still.

During the time when I was writing this book I realised that I hadn't seen Dad for a while, and I was thinking about him a lot. Dad passed away over seven years ago, but he is still a regular visitor … in his spirit form. One day I was sorting through some old jewellery. I've always worn large pieces for my stage work, talks and workshops, particularly sparkly necklaces and jewelled 'collars' (you can see some of my television appearances on YouTube). But in my new Cornish seaside home these larger pieces seemed out of place – too large and glary for casual living. I was searching for smaller and lighter silver pieces to wear and happened upon a small box I hadn't opened in several years. Inside was a small silver ring. I remembered it fondly – Dad used to sell costume jewellery, and 20 years earlier he'd attended a night class on jewellery making to give him a little background on the products he was working on. He'd fashioned the ring out of silver wire, which he'd twisted and soldered together. I still own the jewellery-making tools he used.

I picked it up now and immediately felt his energy attached to the ring. I had a clear image of Dad smiling and encouraging me to put it on. I'd been missing Dad so much over the last few days. Several family members were going through difficulties and

I'd been supporting them. Dad was such a loving man, kind and open to hugs for any occasion, and when I slipped on the ring it was as if he was standing right behind me, hugging me at that very moment. I decided to keep the ring on for a few days. It was bringing me the closeness I needed at that moment. Dad's energy was completely attached to the ring and I wanted to feel him close by as I supported my family in their time of need.

Yet that night I had a visitation experience. I was sitting in a room, watching television. Around me was the whole family, and we were singing along to Michael Bublé blasting out the song 'Everything' on the screen. It was another of Dad's favourite songs. I was sitting next to an open door and didn't initially make the association between the door and the spirit (it being a symbol between one world and the next), but while the whole family sang along to the words about our 'crazy lives' and us being his 'everything', I was aware that I was holding Dad's hand. Dad had giant healing hands as I've mentioned before – warm and loving and comforting. I could feel this healing energy at that moment and the warmth was real. Dad was there. It wasn't the first time he'd come to me in a dream in this way. Dad's healing hands were so important to his family and his arms were always the best place for a hug.

Towards the end of the song I looked around the room. Dad was holding everyone's hand – we had one each (I'm not sure how that worked, as there were more people than hands, but they appeared to be holograms!). The hand I was holding was the only warm one just then, and I was the only one who noticed he was with us. I felt everyone's eyes looking at me at one point, as if they suddenly noticed what I was doing and were asking me, 'Why are you holding a dead man's hand?' But I couldn't answer their unasked questions; I didn't want the spell to break, I didn't want Dad to leave. As the song finished I immediately woke up and realised right away that the song's words reflected Dad's message. He was saying that he was our 'everything' and we were his, that he was everywhere and we made him happy. He was showing his support, letting me know that he was with me while I supported them, my family.

I immediately sent a group message to the family. We always share these experiences – we've told each other about every one of Dad's visits from the other side – so I wasn't surprised when my sister Debbie replied that Dad had appeared to her that night, too. Of course he had! As I stared down at the ring on my hand, Debbie told me she was wearing Dad's watch. She'd spotted it in a drawer the day before and felt compelled to put it on. She confessed that she hadn't seen it for several years but wore it all that day. At night she carefully took it off and slept with it on her night stand. Isn't that a strange 'coincidence'?

Jewellery seems to have the ability to hold the energy vibration of the owner. That person's personality, their vitality, is absorbed by the metals. Picking up on these residue energies in an object is called psychometry. Why not give it a go? Ask to borrow a piece of jewellery from someone. Hold it in your hand and close your eyes. Share your impressions, thoughts, feelings, colours and visions when you do this. It's a fascinating experiment!

Dad had come for a reason that night – one I hadn't yet understood. His visit had a greater meaning than I could have imagined. My cat Tigger was 12 years old. Not old in cat years, but he'd started to suffer with a thyroid problem. This condition can be treated, but there was a part of me that knew Tigger's life was near the end. When my daughters had visited us a few weeks earlier I'd even warned them. It was a kind of inner knowledge, and I'd discussed it with my husband. Tigger had begun taking a great deal of interest in the grassy bank over the road at the end of our drive. His normal good road sense had gone, as he'd taken to searching the bank for insects and small creatures. One day I even saw a car swerve around him and wondered if he might soon get run over.

That night I spoke to my husband John about it. I was worried that even if we treated Tigger for his condition, he would carry on going over the road and would very likely get run over. In my heart of hearts I wanted to do whatever I could for him, but something kept niggling away at me. It was his time. I sighed a deep sigh and said out loud, 'Please, angels, does Tigger want to stay a while longer or is it time to let him go? Can you give me a sign? If he gets run over, I'll know he's ready to leave.'

The next morning I came down to feed Tigger as usual and found him outside, tucked up into the hedge. He'd been knocked down by a car and was limping badly. My heart sank. I realised immediately that Dad had appeared in the dream to prepare me. I carefully carried Tigger into the house wrapped in a towel and gave him a whole stack of cat treats. He even purred as I lay down on the floor next to his head and told him how special he was and what a great pet he had been. We made a strong connection, but the whole time tears were running down my face (as they are right now as I'm typing this out). I stroked him and spoke about all the things we'd done together. Tigger had featured in many of my books and articles – even in my magazine column. He was a celebrity in his own right and he was a very special boy to my family.

I thought the vet might be able to get him well again, but now he would need treating for the accident as well as for the thyroid issue – a long-term condition. I figured that now Tigger had discovered the bank over the road, we'd probably get him well again only for him to get run over again and again, maybe even causing an accident and potentially risking someone else's life. I knew what I had to do.

I called my husband at work and he came home immediately. I stayed with Tigger as the vet gave him his final injection. Death came quickly and I asked to spend a few minutes with him before leaving him behind for good. John had paid the bill and was now waiting for me. 'What would you like to do now?' he asked. I wanted to say goodbye to Tigger properly. 'Let's have a funeral for him right now,' I suggested. He was like a person to us – and any pet owner will completely understand what I'm saying here. Tigger was the king of cats. He was very regal and always held his head up high. Even people who hated cats always loved Tigger. He had the most wonderful personality.

Just a few miles away was a series of beautiful gardens, open to the public. It was a gorgeous day and this seemed like the perfect place to be. As we held hands and entered the garden it felt like the whole place was filled with angels. The first garden had a raised waterfall. A small bird was bathing and we watched, enchanted. The next pool had a large cat statue next to it! And further on we met some butterflies, dragonflies and a squirrel! Ducks and hens roamed the gardens and as we rounded a corner to yet another hidden space we found a pond with a bench nearby, so we sat down to relax for a while and contemplate our huge loss. A large fluffy cat appeared from nowhere and walked right over to be petted. He seemed particularly friendly and rubbed up against our legs! It was quite surreal … enchanting even.

Feeling excited at our magical encounters, we decided to drive to a nearby harbour to eat and relax. The weather was perfect and as soon as we had eaten we walked towards a small beach area, as the tide was out. And then, as we walked towards the harbour wall, a white dove flew out, and this was followed by five more! Could it be another sign? The whole afternoon had been almost dream-like. We stood for a moment on the pebbled shore and then decided it was time to head home. I reached down and picked up a random pebble from the beach and placed it in my pocket without looking at it. Then we headed back to the car. It had been a very sad day, yet at the same time a very wonderful day and a fitting goodbye to Tigger. It was hard to feel upset when we both felt as if the angels had been with us the whole time. It wasn't the right time to say goodbye for us, but it was his chosen day, his time. There was no denying it.

When we arrived home the house seemed unusually quiet, and it dawned on me that we were now a cat-less family. I hung up my coat and remembered the pebble in my pocket. Imagine my surprise when I looked at the pebble and realised it had dark markings on one side. The pebble's outline was in the shape of a cat's face! I grabbed a felt-tipped pen and dotted on a couple of eyes and some whiskers before placing it carefully on the hall table along with some precious crystals. Thank you, angels ... and thank you, Dad! Of course Dad had come to hold my hand; he knew what was happening next in our lives and he'd visited to comfort me in advance.

The next day my daughter rang. She lived a five-hour drive away and had just split up with her fiancé. She wanted to start a new life and asked if she could come and stay for a few months ... and bring her cats with her! I marvelled at the timing. Tigger had been an outdoor cat. With his cat flap, he came and went as he pleased. My daughter's cats were indoor cats. Tigger had made the ultimate sacrifice so that she could come and stay – even though I'd known nothing about what was to come. You can see that having two strange cats come to stay for a few months would not have worked out well, so there was clearly a bigger plan at work. This often seems to be the case. When things appear to 'go wrong' in our lives, the angels know there is more going on behind the scenes.

We mere humans, on the other hand, don't always know what is going to happen next. I knew that Dad had appeared in the dream to hold my hand because he knew that life was going to be challenging just a little further along the line. My daughter settled in well, and her cats did, too (one of them has just popped into my writing room!). But that is not the end of the story. A week after Tigger passed on I had a dream visitation from him. In my dream I was watching television and felt the cat jump up beside me. I leaned over to stroke him and as my hand touched his fur I became lucid and aware. I knew immediately that this was a spirit visit from Tigger. I could feel him as if he were still alive. He'd come to let me know he was okay. He'd come to say goodbye.

Although this book is about angels visiting us on special occasions, I want you to know that angels and the spirits of our loved ones are with us all year long. To us, this was a special occasion, a time when the family missed their father and grandfather, when they longed for the healing touch of his hands and the hug that represented his love. During a difficult time in our lives he drew close to show his never-ending support. Dad was our angel and in so many ways he never left us.

This next experience is from Angie. She wrote to ask for some advice, but at the same time shared her story with me. She explained, 'I'm currently reading your book, *An Angel by My Side*, in which lots of people have spoken about dream visitations.' (A theme of this book, too.) Angie didn't know her biological dad until she was 10. Another man brought her up, and she called him Dad. In her eyes he was her father and she didn't know any different until her mum told her the truth 25 years ago. It was at this time that she met Brett for the first time – her biological dad.

Angie felt no connection with him, and didn't like him as much as she felt she should. He wasn't a horrible man, but she felt she just didn't 'gel' with him. They had an intermittent relationship for years. Then, when she became pregnant with her first child, she wrote to him to tell him that she didn't want her child to be confused over the relationship and had therefore decided to cut all ties with him. Angie confided that she'd never once called him Dad and only referred to him by his first name.

She wanted the man who had brought her up, whom she considered to be her dad, to be the grand-dad to her child – he'd earned that title. He'd played the role of father through good times and bad, and had always felt uncomfortable at her having contact with Brett. 'My dad saw me as his own child and not Brett's,' Angie says.

Time passed and Angie carried on with life; her little girl loved her granddad very much. Then she became pregnant again with her second child. Harry was born in 2008. When Harry was a few months old Angie saw Brett in her road. He stopped his van to talk to her but she quickly ushered the children indoors and pretended she didn't see him. That October, Brett died. When she was told the news she says she felt gutted. Sad. This was confusing, because she was the one who had chosen not to have contact.

That night, as she lay in the bath, she cried for this man she had hardly known, but at the same time she felt a fraud because she hadn't wanted the kids to know about Brett, and she herself hadn't been bothered about him ... At least that's what she thought.

Angie did attend his funeral in the hope that it would bring her some closure, and once more she cried. For the first time she saw photographs of him as a young man. He was smiling, laughing – a handsome man – and she felt sad that she hadn't known him at that time. She explained, 'I felt like I'd made the wrong choices with him. And now it was too late and I couldn't change a single thing.' In her head she often thinks of Brett and apologises for her choices. She now wishes she hadn't been so forthright and bitter.

About a year ago Angie had a dream. In it she was sitting in a coffee shop with her mum. Brett walked in and she realised immediately how happy she was to see him. They talked and laughed (although she couldn't remember what about afterwards), and it was the easiest conversation she'd ever had with him. She also remembers a lady with blue eyes and blonde wavy hair who walked past them and stopped. She smiled and said, 'You have the same cheekbones as your dad ...' As they all left the coffee shop, Angie said, 'Goodbye, Dad,' for the first and last time. Still in the dream, they got into their car and drove away. As she was driving, Angie turned to her mum and said how nice it was that she had finally felt able to call him Dad – but for the first time it had felt as if he really was her dad.

It's never too late for closure – it's one of the reasons why deceased loved ones come back from the other side of life. Was the lady with the blue eyes Brett's guardian angel, come to support her charge as he said a final goodbye to his daughter? Maybe. We'll never know.

My Dear Readers,

Whatever the occasion in your life, whether it's an anniversary, a birthday, Christmas, Easter or something else entirely, remember that you can always ask for help from your loving guardian angels. Our angels will show that they are close, and may even send a deceased family member over for support and the love that you miss and need at that very moment. The afterlife is ever present. Love never dies, and support and affection is always around if we need it.

We've discovered that angels can escort our loved ones forward from the other side, seemingly lending their energy to the visiting spirit and helping to create a bridge from one side to the other. We've seen how they can intervene in love, and urge living friends to contact us. They can bring us many signs to show they are around, and we've covered just a few examples in this little volume. White feathers are a familiar and popular calling card, but spirits have also rung bells, called out our names, flickered lights and appeared in dream visits. They sometimes bring living creatures to comfort us; as we've seen, robins and butterflies seem particularly popular.

I've experienced many of these things for myself, and if you've read any of my earlier works you'll know that I began writing books of angel and afterlife experiences following some angelic encounters of my own, starting right back when I was a child. I've had numerous spirit and angelic visitations during dreams and experienced all manner of random (and usually unexplained) psychic phenomena. As I explained earlier, I've heard spirits (or angels) call my name, I've picked up information about people psychically (connecting to their aura or body energy) and even about strangers' deceased loved ones. Occasionally I get premonitions about things to come in my own life and in the lives of the people around me. I regularly (almost daily) connect with my husband telepathically (a mind-to-mind connection where words are not spoken). I've been warned of danger and I've received good news. I've found I can read people's energy and pick up information for them using angel cards, and on many occasions I've felt physical and mental connections with my loved ones on the other side of life.

A Christmas Angel

Strangest of all, I don't really understand how any of this works. But I'm not sure that even matters. What is really important is to keep an open mind about these things. Angels surely exist and, without a doubt, life continues after the death of the physical body. So much of our life is planned before we are born, and many of the things we experience are chosen by the soul so that we can learn lessons and grow.

Whatever situation you find yourself in, remember that you are never alone. Each of us has our own guardian angel. This is no make-believe or fairy tale. In my books and in the course of my own research over 13 years or so, I've personally come across thousands and thousands of people who have had these types of spiritual and psychic encounters. Life is not the logical and straight-forward experience we think it is. I'm sure if you look back over your own life, you'll recall weird moments that have happened and for which you had no explanation. Life can be strange and magical and wonderful.

Have you ever felt a loved one or an angel around you during a special moment in your life? I'd love to hear from you if you have. Remember that just because we can't see them, it doesn't mean they aren't right there with you. You might hear them, sense them or even smell them. Always remember to invite your deceased loved ones to family events.

Jacky Newcomb

I hope you have enjoyed reading about angels in this book. I've written piles more books and I know you'll enjoy them, too. If you'd like to find out more about my work, you are welcome to visit my website. You'll also find me on Twitter and Facebook.

Until next time,

Jacky Newcomb,

'The Angel Lady' xx

www.JackyNewcomb.com